Get-Set-Sketch!

Secrets of Pen and Ink Sketching
Unleashed!

ABOUT THE AUTHOR

Shirish is a self-taught artist based in a very populous city called Pune, in a very populous country called India.

Shirish has worked in the thriving IT Industry for more than two decades. But he is an artist by heart. Sketching, painting and teaching art is Shirish's first, second and third love (not necessarily in that sequence!).

Shirish dabbles in various subjects such as landscapes, portraits, figure studies and abstracts. He works in various media like Pen & Inks, Watercolors, Oils, Acrylics and Spray Paints.

Shirish has participated in many art exhibitions, and his sketches and paintings are present in private collections in India and various other countries.

Shirish has published some very successful video courses on Udemy.com and SkillShare.com, which he produces himself. These courses have helped thousands of students worldwide learn the intricacies of sketching and painting.

Shirish has such undying passion for teaching art that it has manifested into many forms in the recent past, including live workshops, video trainings, and now in the form of this book.

Shirish Deshpande

Get-Set-Sketch!

Secrets of Pen & Ink Sketching Unleashed!

First Edition

ISBN-13:978-1725571143
ISBN-10: 1725571145

Meet the Author here:

Email: shirishauthor@gmail.com

Website: http://www.HuesAndTones.net/home.html

Sign up for my newsletter and get the ebook and printable PDF versions of my adult coloring book "Dystopian Encounters – Wave 1" absolutely free!

You will also get a handy PDF guide to the Materials for Pen and Ink Sketching. Get my exclusive sketching and painting tips directly delivered to your mailbox.

(I will neither spam your mailbox, nor share your email ID with anyone else, I promise).

YouTube: https://www.youtube.com/c/huesandtones

Facebook Page: HuesAndTones

Instagram: HuesAndTones1

Pinterest: https://in.pinterest.com/sd2313/

Video Courses:

https://www.udemy.com/user/shirish-deshpande-3/

https://www.skillshare.com/user/huesandtones

Table of Contents

INTRODUCTION

I am glad you made it this far!

Welcome to "Get-Set-Sketch!", a turbocharged guide to jumpstart your pen and ink sketching experience.

The beauty of pen and ink as a medium is that - it is anytime, anywhere! There's no tiresome cleanup afterwards, the materials are (mostly) affordable, and possibilities are endless.

In this book, we will together embark on a magical journey through the realm of inks to create stunning sketches.

So, let's get inking!

Who is this Book for?

- Are you a beginner to the art of sketching? Have you been away from sketching for a greater part of your life?

- Are you a passionate artist, who wants to enhance your skills?

- Are you afraid of sketching?

- Are you excited by the mere thought of sketching?

- Are you a hobby artist or a professional?

Then this book is for you! Yes... YOU!

Before We Begin …

If you are intimidated by sketching, I totally understand you! Me too have experienced firsthand, how traditional methods and rules of art teaching in schools kill the creativity of students.

Everyone is a born artist. The problem is that most people forget this fact as they grow up.

My mission is to rekindle that creativity and love for art, which every one of us has.

After all, art is THE one quality that separates us from animals.

What do you need to have to learn Sketching?

- Love of art

- An open mind

- An unchained imagination

- Loads of enthusiasm

- Loads of enthusiasm

    and...

- *Loads of enthusiasm*

THE BEGINNER'S DILEMMA

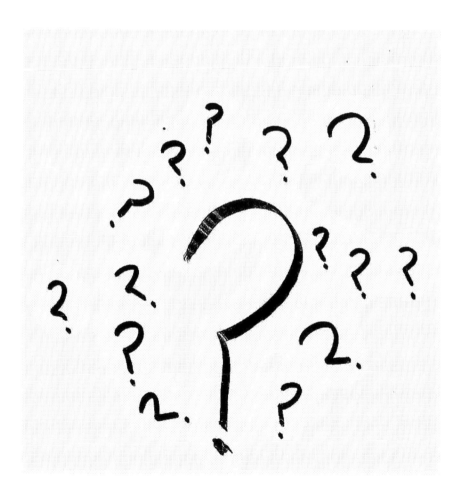

What is a good sketch?

Let's start with a basic question. What is a good piece of art?

Let's go to even more basic level. What is art?

Ask this question to a hundred people, and you will get a hundred answers. But one thing is certain - art invokes feelings in us. Those feelings may be happy, sad, erotic, ecstatic, fearful or even grotesque.

Any kind of art form, be it auditory, visual or sensory, is a success only when it can invoke feelings in the audience (hopefully the same kind of feelings it's intended to invoke!)

So, let's come back to our original question. What is good art?

Or, to keep us closer to the subject of this book, what is a good sketch?

The most common compliment I get for my sketches/paintings are to the tune of "This looks so real" or better yet, "This looks exactly like a photograph".

And this gem heard recently – "Your sketches are posing a serious competition to the camera!"

SERIOUSLY??

These kinds of comments make me cringe!

Why?

Because though the intentions of these well-wishers are noble, they are unknowingly insulting my sketches!

A sketch is never intended to mimic reality. We have cameras for that!

A sketch is supposed to enhance reality. A sketch is a unique expression of the sketcher on a subject.

A photographer has only so much control over what the camera sees and captures. He/she may enhance the photograph later and add/remove elements as they suit the purpose.

A sketcher has the freedom to choose the elements he/she wants to be part of the sketch at the making stage itself.

A sketcher even has the freedom to sketch only part of a scene and declare the sketch as finished!

So, all the present and would be sketchers out there… repeat this mantra with me.

I will never try to mimic a photograph

I will never try to mimic a photograph

I will never try to mimic a photograph

See, haven't you already started feeling better? Isn't that a huge burden off your chest?

Let's make you feel even better.

Have a look at this photograph, and the sketch based on this photograph. Which one looks better?

See what I mean?

But I couldn't draw a straight line if my life depended on it

Let me ask you another question. Can you read and write? If you are reading this, I think you can!

Then you can sketch.

Let me elaborate.

Have a look at the following word. What does it say?

"F L O W E R"

Did you just read this word as "flower"? Did you visualize a flower as you read this? Why?

Why did you visualize this word as flower, and not as a rock, or brick, or a pancake?

Because you saw a bunch of lines and circles, which you interpreted as letters, which you in turn used to form a word, and mentally translated it into a very real object.

And every one of us can write this word, right? Every one of us can draw those lines and circles which represent an object.

Now all we must do is draw some lines and circles which are visually closer to the reality!

Since this main mental block is out of the way, let's see how we can quickly progress from Abstraction to Reality… that is from...

"F L O W E R"

to

Abstraction vs. Reality

Abstraction is a representation of an object in artistic form.

The extreme form of abstraction, which we use all the time without ever realizing it, is called writing.

Sketching falls somewhere between hyper realism (photograph/photorealistic painting) and total abstraction (writing).

The degree to which the sketch will have that abstraction is totally up to you.

But one must follow certain "rules" while deciding this abstraction.

Abstraction

Realism

FLOWER

"Rules" of Sketching

Two basic rules govern sketching and art in general.

These are *highly authentic, very rigid, and irrefutable* rules.

You are not allowed to break or bend these rules *under any circumstances*!

If you want to be a sketcher, amateur or professional, you must understand and internalize these rules.

Are you ready to unveil these rules?

Let's say it then.

Rule #1 is .. (drumroll please) that THERE ARE NO RULES!

And Rule#2 is … If you ever start feeling constipated about the "rules" of art, refer to rule #1!

That's it. Now that we have covered the absolute rules of art, let's delve deeper into sketching.

LEARNING TO "SEE"

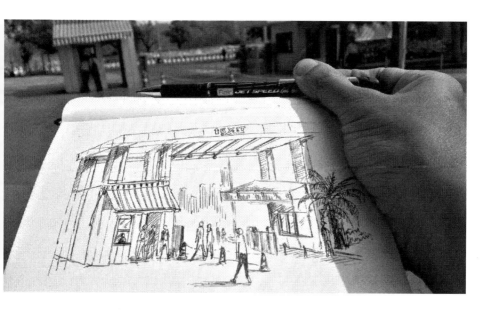

Have you ever wondered how two people see exactly the same stuff, but one finds it insipid, while the other one finds it inspiring?

Have you heard people complaining that they really, really would like to sketch, but don't find any inspiration for sketching?

And have you seen someone trying to sketch a lion, but which got sketched out looking like a donkey?

What's the difference between the way an average person sketches and an artist would sketch? Is there such a remarkable difference in skills?

Yes, but not always!

The difference begins with the way both these people "see" things around them.

But I see things all the time, you may say.

Yes, I agree that you see things, but do you really "see" things?

Before you panic, let me explain.

Have a look at this picture. What do you see?

Do you see a building?

If yes, you may not be able to sketch this building!

Why? You may ask.

Because you are not "seeing" the object (building in this case) that you want to sketch the way a sketcher sees it.

If you want to sketch this building, you need to see it differently.

There are three ways of "seeing" an object as a sketcher, and we need to learn all three.

Way 1 – See the shapes

Look at the object as a collection of broad shapes. Do you see rectangles?

Polygons? Circles? Squares? Triangles?

Way 2 – See the shadows

Look at the object as a collection of light and shadow shapes.

In this picture above, I have marked

    a> The darkest shadows as pure black (both the right facing the walls),

    b> Middle tone shadows as grey (middle wall facing us),

    c> Lightest shadows as very light grey (the leftmost wall).

Way 3 – See the textures

Here I have marked the part of the building with brickwork in black.

Way 3 – See the textures (continued)

Then there's a different texture for various glass windows with their wooden frames.

Way 3 – See the textures (continued)

And the plants partially covering the walls have their own unique texture.

So far we learned that in order to sketch any object, we need to "see" the following three things:

a. Shapes

b. Shadows (and light)

c. Textures

Now let's learn about some materials we can use for pen and ink sketching.

MATERIALS

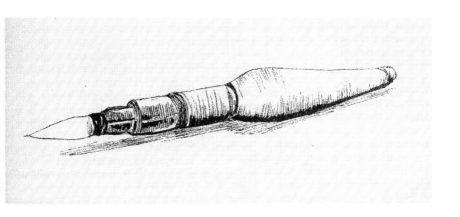

For basic sketching, you need only two things… a blank paper and a ballpoint pen/gel pen.

However, we artists are never satisfied with limited materials. We always want more!

So, here's a list of all the materials that I use for pen and ink sketching.

This does not mean this is the exhaustive list of materials.

The list of materials, just like the list of subjects, is virtually endless. But I will try to provide a starting point for your next shopping list.

Pencil, Eraser and Sharpener

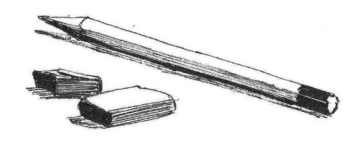

Although entire sketches can be done using a pencil, here I will focus on using a pencil to do rough work for a complete pen and ink sketch.

Pencils are of three types:

a. "H" type – these are hard pencils which produce very light shades.

b. "B" type – very soft pencils which create very dark shades.

c. "HB" type – somewhere in between "H" and "B".

Since I use pencils only for rough work in a pen and ink sketch, my intention is to erase these lines later. So I prefer either "H" or "HB" type pencils.

Is this how I do it? – Yes

Does it have to be done this way? – Refer to Rule #1 at the end of "The Beginner's Dilemma" chapter!

Pens

There are many choices for pens, and each has their own advantages:

Ball point pens/Gel pens – They are very cheap, available in assorted colors and easily available.

When using these pens, make sure you keep a spare rag/rough paper nearby. These pens tend to accumulate ink near their tips, which may result in ugly dots on the sketch.

Make sure you keep wiping the pen tip periodically before, after and during sketching.

I suggest having a white ink ballpoint pen handy as well. These are useful in making corrections, as well as sketching light parts over dark areas.

Here's a sketch done entirely using a ballpoint pen.

Technical Pens

These pens are especially made for sketching. They have in-built ink reservoirs. They are available in various tip sizes and I highly recommend them to anyone who is serious about pen & ink sketching.

There are various brands of technical pens available. Some well known brand names are - Sakura Pigma Micron, Faber-Castell, Brustro, Artliner, Staedtler etc.

You may start with a set of various nib sizes, and then try out various brands as you progress. The feel of each pen may vary, and you would want to test out various brands before settling on one.

These technical pens are available in assorted colors as well.

Here's a sketch done entirely using technical pens.

Brush Tip Pens

These pens are similar to technical pens, but they have a brush tip instead of a hard nib. They have in in-built ink reservoir, just like technical pens.

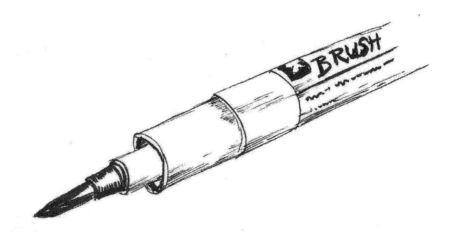

Brush tip pens are especially useful in creating "organic" looking lines. They can also be used to darken large portions of a sketch. More on that later in this chapter.

Brush tip pens are excellent in creating an ink effect without using water.

Brush tip pens are available in assorted colors.

Here's an example of a sketch done mostly using a brush tip pen. The fine fur on the nose and head is sketched using technical pens.

Acrylic Inks:

Inks of various brands and thicknesses are available for sketching.
recommend any ink which is thick and lightfast.

I use inks from two brands, Daler Rowney and Sumi. I have great
results with both of these. However, you may want to try out
different brands before you settle on one or more.

Inks can be applied with watercolor brushes, dip pens, quills, or
even twigs! The tools available to apply ink on paper are limited
only by your imagination.

These inks are completely waterproof once dry, so they can be applied along with watercolors as well.

Acrylic inks are also available in assorted colors.

Here is an example of inks applied using a dry twig.

Water Brushes:

These brushes have an in-built water reservoir.

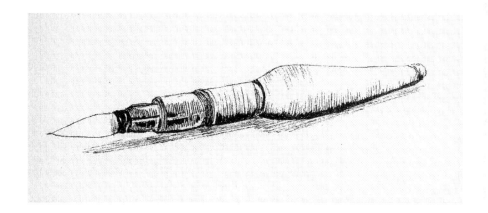

These brushes are especially useful when applying thin washes over sketches to depict soft shadows. The reservoir can be squeezed to allow water to flow into the brush tip.

The amount of water can be controlled to decide on the amount of ink being dispensed.

Here's an example of a sketch where water brush was used to apply grey shades.

Sketching paper:

The beauty of pen and ink medium is that it can be practiced anywhere.

Even a paper napkin at a restaurant table is enough for a pen sketch.

However, the best results can be obtained by using the right kind of paper for the right kind of sketch.

I will tell you about some of the papers that I have used.

While selecting a paper, you need to consider the following things.

    a> Paper thickness
    b> Paper texture

Paper thickness is measured in GSM (Grams per square meter). Without going into details, just understand that the more GSM value is specified for a paper, the thicker it is.

Typical sketchbook papers are available from 50 GSM all the way upwards of 400 GSM thicknesses.

Smaller GSM papers (70-120 GSM) are ok for ball point/technical pen work. But these papers tend to buckle when using water-based inks, or water colors. Inks and watercolors also tend to seep through these thin papers.

Bigger GSM value papers (upward of 250 GSM) are preferably used for ink and watercolor work.

I typically use 70-120 GSM papers for pen work, and 250-300 GSM Canson/Fabriano papers for inks/watercolor work. I also sometime use Poster Board papers for sketching. They are thick as well as smooth for penwork.

Paper smoothness/roughness can be used to create various textures in the sketch.

Technical pens work better on smooth papers, like Bristol boards or Poster boards.

Watercolors/inks work better on textured/rough papers.

This sketch was done on an ultra smooth Bristol paper (120 GSM) using only technical pens. Observe the textures created using pen here.

This sketch was done on a semi-textured Canson paper (250 GSM) using technical pens and black India ink. Observe how the paper texture has been used to create rough stone effect.

SHADING
TECHNIQUES

I welcome thee to the dark side!

Pen and ink sketching is all about understanding and exploiting light and dark shades. These are also called "values" in artist-speak.

So, in the rest of the book, we will use the words "values" and "shades" interchangeably.

Since we will be (initially) working in monochrome, it's important to understand how to use values, so our sketches make some sense to the viewers.

Values are also very important, since we are sketching 3D objects onto a 2D surface (a flat paper).

Have a look at the following pictures. Which of them looks 3D?

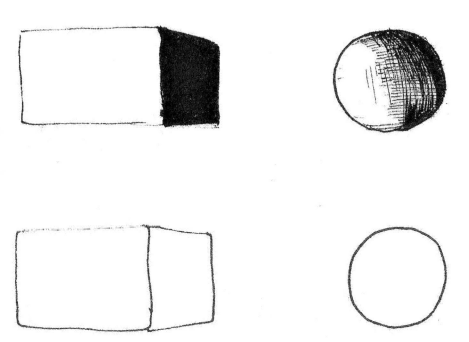

But before we start learning to shade…

Go back to the list of materials I specified in the "Materials" chapter.

Did I mention a ruler there?

I didn't?

"Why?", you may ask.

Because I neither use, nor advocate using a ruler while sketching.

The reason will become clear after we learn some shading. Believe me, there's an airtight reason for this.

But then what is the secret of drawing straight lines as in this picture?

Before learning that secret, let's see where we normally go wrong.

Most people, while sketching, move their palm using their wrist as the pivot. This severely restricts the range of motion for the hand.

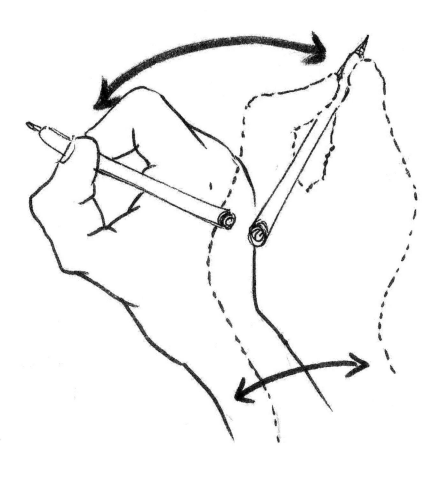

The correct way is to move the hand using the elbow as the pivot.

This enables free hand movement and allows a greater range of motion.

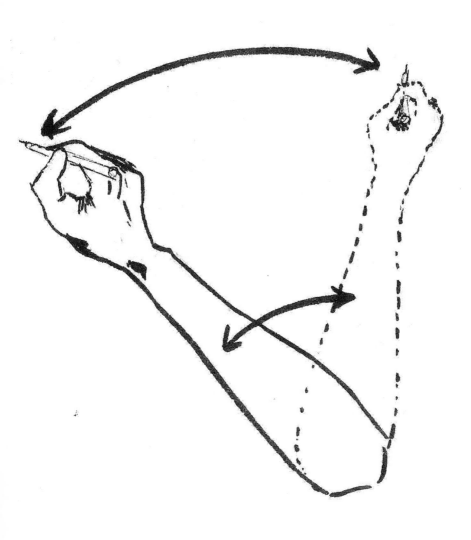

Now try drawing a straight line using the technique shown on the previous page.

Go on, I will be waiting right here.

Was the line absolutely straight? No? Did you expect it to be on your first attempt?

What matters is if the line was better than your previous effort.

If yes, that's good enough. If no, you may be using the hand movement incorrectly.

Does the line even need to be straight? Not necessarily.

Why? Because if the lines are drawn perfectly straight using a ruler, they will stick out like sore thumbs among all the hand drawn hatching lines (which we will cover on the next page itself).

And if you are thinking of drawing the hatching lines using a ruler, I wish thee luck for your marathon sketch!

Try drawing a straight line one more time. Don't get hung up on the line if the line is still crooked. You will improve as we go along in the next chapters.

Shading Technique #1: Hatching

Hatching is a very simple shading technique where we draw (almost) parallel lines which are (almost always) equidistant.

That was less of an artistic sentence and more of a legal one!

Why so many disclaimers?

Because of the "rules" we talked about at the end of "The Beginner's Dilemma" chapter.

Let's see how hatching is done.

Have a look at the various hatched areas below:

As you can observe here, the hatching lines are parallel, but the lines in the hatched areas on the top-left and bottom-right of the page differ.

Here, the lines are gradually getting closer and denser.

You can draw denser lines to indicate darker shades, or distant lines to indicate light shades.

Now go ahead and do some practice drawing such hatching lines using a pen. (No, no, no. Not pencil. Use a pen. No cheating!)

Just one precaution: When doing hatching, at the end of every line, consciously lift your hand before you start drawing the next line. Otherwise the lines will end up with such ugly "hooks".

Remember, at this stage, technique is more important. Speed is secondary!

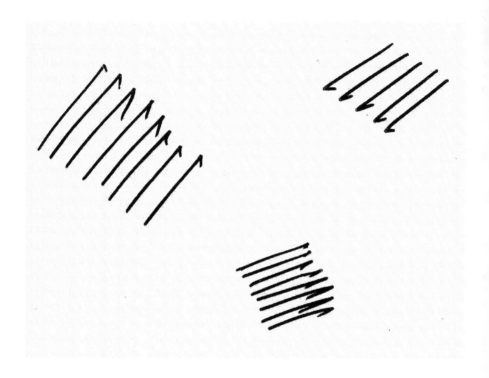

Now go ahead. Do some practice and go on to the next chapter.

Here's an example of hatching being used in the shading:

Shading Technique #2: Cross-hatching

Cross-hatching means doing hatching in more than one direction over one another. That's it. Really!

See some examples of cross hatching below, and you will understand.

You can do horizontal hatching and then vertical hatching on top.

Or you can do diagonal hatching.

Or you can combine everything.

Are there any rules? Oh yess. See the end of "The Beginner's Dilemma" chapter for rules!

Now do some practice of cross hatching. Then we will explore the next shading technique.

Here's an example of cross hatching used in shading

Shading Technique #3: Contour shading

This is a variant of all the hatching techniques.

It's extremely useful to show the objects as 3D.

Let's see with an example.

Let's have a pillar and assume that the light falls on this pillar from right side. So the part of pillar on the left side should be in the shadow.

But if we use simple hatching/cross-hatching to shade this pillar, will this look 3D? You bet it won't! It will look flat, like this picture of the left.

Why? Because the pillar has a horizontal curve, which is lost here

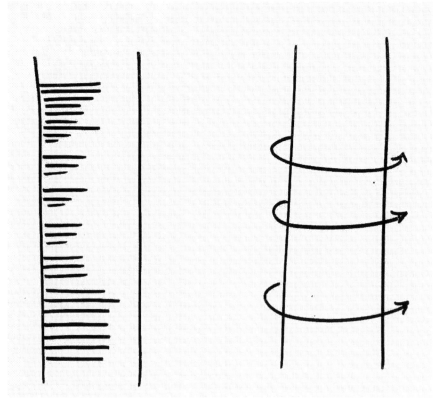

But what if we sketch the horizontal hatching lines along the curve of the pillar? Now does it automatically bring out that curve? Ohh yes!

Just one precaution: When drawing the curvy lines, pretend that you are covering the whole area from left to right (shown as dotted part of the hatching lines). Else the hatching lines will "stab" the object as shown on the right!

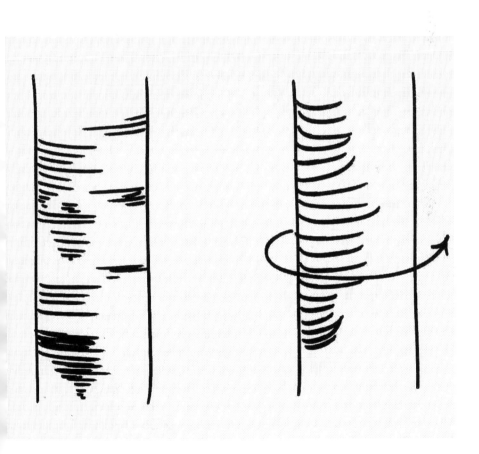

Here's an example of a sketch done with contour technique.

Shading Technique #4: Stippling

Stippling is a technique where one can create shades using a combination of dots.

The denser the dots, darker the values.

Make sure the pen is held perfectly vertical to the paper and is lifted after every dot.

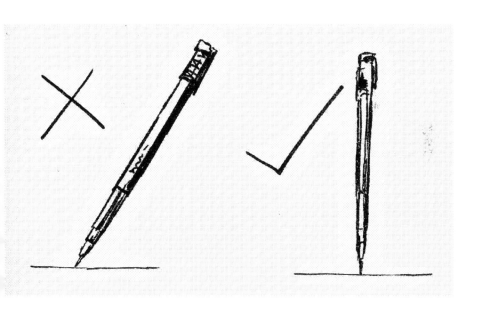

Now do some practice with stippling, as shown below. Try doing stippling with dense dots, as well as light dots. Try various combinations. After that, we move to the next technique.

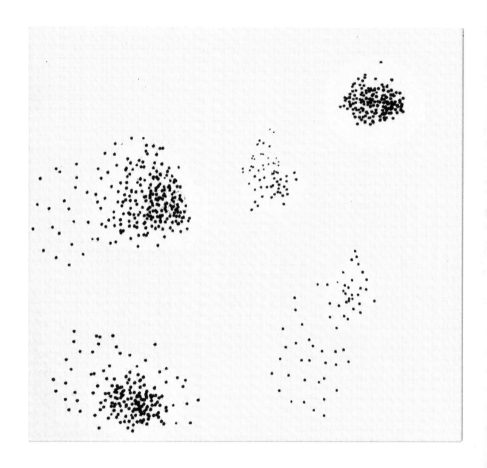

Here's an example (part of a) sketch done with the stippling technique.

Shading Technique #5: Random

Random is a shading technique which appears very simple.

And it is, if used correctly.

Random shading is exactly what it sounds like, random.

But when doing random shading, one must keep in mind the shape of the object over which this shading is being done.

Below, I have shown some examples of random shading. I have also given some practical examples like trees and clouds.

When doing random shading, I will insist that you first mark the area with dotted lines (as shown here), or pencil, so that you don't go overboard.

Believe me, I am speaking from experience!

Here's an example of a sketch which heavily uses random technique for foliage.

That's it about shading techniques with pen.

We will learn about shading with inks when we reach the inks part.

For now, we will see how choosing different shading techniques affects the sketch.

Here's an example of a sketch shaded with cross hatching, and the same sketch shaded with stippling technique.

Here are these same sketches zoomed in:

Are there any rules about which shading techniques should be used under which conditions?

Yes, the same rules from "The Beginner's Dilemma" chapter apply!

However, no harm understanding a few rules of thumb.

When using hatching/cross hatching together, use cross hatching for darker shades (common sense, I know. Still…)

You may use more than one shading technique in the same area. Totally ok. We will see some examples soon.

Do as your gut feeling tells you.

This is art, not a freaking math exam!

Headache for you: Have a look at this sketch and see if you can find out all the shading techniques used.

USING INK FOR SHADING

Using inks directly to shade sketches is such a big topic that I found it necessary to devote a separate chapter for this one technique.

How should one decide whether to use pens or inks for shading?

To answer that… I will again stress this: *This is not a freaking math exam! It's art. You decide by your gut feeling.*

And the available materials, of course.

What materials does one require for ink shading?

For starters, an ink bottle. I have suggested a few types of inks in the Materials section. However, you are free to use any brand you are comfortable with.

If you don't know which ink brand you are comfortable with, you need to try out some brands before you settle on one.

Search for "India ink" or "acrylic ink" in the online stores or your local art store.

You will need a few watercolor brushes of various sizes (three-four synthetic brushes are enough), a water brush would be an added advantage.

Keep a small pot containing water handy for washing the brushes. Keep some soft tissue papers handy to wipe the brushes.

I also like to use a toothbrush for adding some interesting effects to the sketch. Here's one example. Look at the interesting effect it has created at the bottom of the hut.

Of course, the materials that you can use have no limits. You may use twigs, toothpicks, tissue papers, plastic sheets, tooth brushes, fingers, or any other tools you may think of.

You may use a brush tipped pen to create the same effect as a brush creating a dark shade.

Both pens and inks have their own beauty. So one cannot really say that one of them is better than the other.

But when it comes to shading large areas, using inks decidedly reduces one's efforts.

Inks, along with brushes and other tools, creates more "organic" lines, while pens create more uniform lines.

Again, one is not better than the other. You may use both in combination as well for their advantages.

You can either use ink to create very dark shades…

…or grey tones

Both these methods have their own advantages. One is not necessarily better than the other.

Whether to use pens, inks with dark shades, or inks with grey tones, or a combination of these, is totally up to your gut feeling and the materials available.

I think I have hammered this point of "gut feeling" enough in your head now.

So over to action. Let's quit thinking and start inking!

These are how the various strokes look.

Now let's learn in detail how to sketch various objects using pen and inks. We will cover various topics and learn about specific shading methods used for creating textures.

Let's start with a topic where there's very low probability to go wrong!

TREES, GRASS AND SHRUBS

In this chapter, we will cover several topics of sketching with pens and inks.

There are practically infinite varieties of trees, shrubs and assorted plants on this planet.

Trees are also a very interesting topic to sketch.

Tree and shrub leaves pose an interesting challenge to sketch, because sketching every leaf is not practical, and sketching just the outline is not enough!

Tree barks present interesting challenges (and opportunities) to experiment with various textures.

Here, I have shown tree bark (from left) in exquisitely detailed and somewhat less detailed.

Here's a tree shown completely silhouetted.

Note that there are gaps between the leaves. These are called "sky holes", and they should be left out in leaves to make the sketch more believable.

Never fill up the entire area of the tree canopy.

How much detail you want to put into your sketch depends on the topic at hand, sketch composition, time at hand, and of course, the artist's mood.

Artist's mood? Is such a thing even important? Hell yeh!

But anyway, speaking of trees...

The best way to practice sketching trees is to observe the plant life around you and sketch it.

Remember to use the contour method of shading to emphasize textures. The tree trunks are typically cylindrical in shape, and the curve of the bark must be emphasized while drawing texture.

Below, I have shown a few examples of tree bark. Of course, just like anything in nature, the varieties are endless.

See how a few simple contour strokes, combined with light and dark areas, pop out the volume and rough texture of the bark.

This is a quick sketch of the trunk of a (date) palm tree. See how the interlocking parts of the bark are indicated with few dark strokes.

When sketching trees, focus on the overall effect, not on too many details.

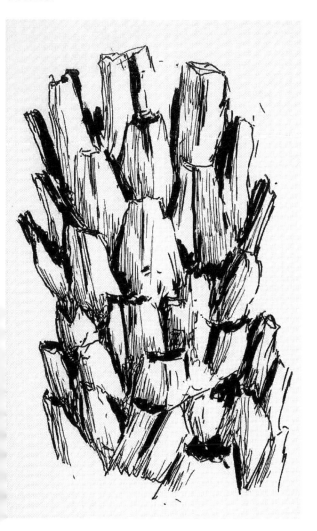

Trees are often juxtaposed against grass/other trees or other objects. Here, the two trunks on the foreground, along with some grass, act as the main subjects of interest.

To highlight them, and push everything else in the background, I have used vertical hatching strokes.

Vertical hatching strokes are super useful when sketching out-of-focus backgrounds.

I have used the same kind of strokes in the "headache" exercise I gave you at the end of "Shading Techniques" chapter. There was too much visual clutter in this image. There's a background chain link fence, and two bamboo sticks in the foreground, along with a slew of plants.

To get better visual clarity, I have selectively used dark shades, and kept details of leaves in some areas to a minimum.

Also, I took special care to make sure lines in the background fence were relatively straight. Rarely are lines so straight in the nature, and that creates a stark contrast between this artificial object and natural plants.

This is part of a sketch where the contour lines for bark texture are juxtaposed against the random strokes for leaves.

Observe again how the contrast between various shading techniques helps in visual clarity to a sketch which would otherwise have been much cluttered.

Also see how white spaces are important in bringing about the visual clarity.

Without white spaces, this sketch would be a jumble of unrecognizable pen strokes.

White spaces are as important as pen/ink work in a sketch.

STONES AND ROCKS

Stones and rocks are another "safe" subject to draw, which means you don't need as much accuracy as say portraits or buildings.

However, we need to be much more aware of values when sketching rocks.

Rocks are of different types like hard rocks, rocks with sharp edges, smooth pebbles, grainy rocks etc.

Just like trees and shrubs, there are practically infinite varieties of rocks.

We will see how to sketch a few of these varieties.

Rock with hard edges - This is a fun type of rock to draw, since there are so many opportunities to draw hard edges and dark spaces in the nooks and crevices.

Note the fine lines drawn on the surface of rocks. It's important not to overdo drawing these to avoid clutter.

Here's another example of rough rocks with some moss on them.

Notice how the moss is represented using stippling.

Big rocks in arid regions - These are intentionally shaded very dark in the shadow region so that the white part appears brighter.

These rocks have comparatively smoother surfaces but have a lot of cracks and nooks.

Notice the minimal detailing, and mostly dark values in the shadow region.

Smooth pebbles - The smoothness is emphasized by minimal shading.

However, the rocks are not entirely "glass smooth". They have fine freckle-like patterns on them. These patterns are shown using stippling. The rougher patches on the rocks are shown using hatching/cross hatching.

ANIMAL FUR

While sketching animal fur, we use a type of stroke which is a variant of hatching.

This type of stroke is called "criss-cross hatching".

This hatching is similar to what we use for the grass.

While using criss-cross hatching to sketch animal fur, remember these two important points:

1. Animal fur radiates out from animal bodies/faces.
2. There's no one uniform patch of fur on an animal. Instead, there are various clumps of fur.

In this Panda sketch, observe how the fur on the face appears to be radiating towards the extremities of the face.

Also note how much space is kept empty! It's never too much to emphasize that white spaces are as important as the ink itself.

In this lion sketch below, see how the criss-cross pen strokes radiate outward to indicate the mane.

The cross-hatching strokes drawn with the same pen, however, indicate non-hairy areas on the face.

Isn't it interesting that just changing the style of strokes suddenly makes us look at the areas as having different textures?

This is the magic of contrast! In this case, it's the contrast between two shading techniques (criss-cross and cross-hatching).

One can use the brush + pens combination to depict fur as well, as shown in these two examples. Here, I have used light grey shades, followed by fine criss-cross lines.

WOOD

Wood, as used in the construction of houses, barns and doors, is an interesting subject to sketch.

Shading for bringing out the texture in wood is easy. I will show it below.

However, the sketch will really come out well when one understands the character of the place beyond the simple looking wood.

Have a look at this wooden door and tell me if you don't just see the wood, but also decades of human memories and emotions attached to this door!

This is not just a door, it's a story of the place!

I am getting emotional here!

Give me a couple of minutes and I will be back (sob).

So… where was I?

Ahh, I was going to tell you how to draw the wood texture.

Right!

So here's the secret. Ready?

Look at this picture of a few wooden planks side by side.

You can notice 2 types of strokes here:

1. Those running vertically along the length of the wood. These are vertical and broken. Also notice that even though they are parallel to each other, no two adjacent strokes are the same in length.

   The strokes are also slightly wavy, rather than straight.

2. Those which are semi-circular, are having the legacy of the tree from which the wood is extracted. Again notice how the strokes are left kinda halfway.

Apart from these, there are some small holes in the wood. Together these factors provide a natural feel to the wood sketch.

Because the gaps between planks are vertical, and the strokes on the planks are also vertical, how do we visually separate the planks?

They are separated from each other by thickening the gaps between planks. Here we are using dark values to indicate separation between planks and light values for the texture on the planks themselves.

On top of the texture lines are thin strokes to indicate shadows.

One important thing to always keep in mind… Never give in to the temptation of doing "some more texturing". See the picture below for the example of how to draw minimum texture on the wood.

Here's a close look at the wooden door

WATER

Water can be sketched in various forms like a flowing river, calm lake, or stormy sea.

Depending on the way one wants to portray the water body, the style of sketching will change.

One important difference when sketching water – Water's shape and behavior is defined by what is around the water. The actual water may contain few details.

Here the real magic of white spaces is revealed!

Calm Water

When sketching calm water, less is more!

Don't sketch everything, let the viewer's mind fill in the details.

Look at the sketch above. You can easily make out the presence of water due to reflections.

Some horizontal strokes with pens and white pen are enough to indicate ripples on the water.

Again, don't overdo sketching those ripples.

Waterfall

Waterfalls have bubbling, white water.

When sketching a waterfall using pen and inks, give more emphasis on the area surrounding the waterfall, rather than the waterfall itself.

Some strategically placed lines within the main body of the waterfall are enough to indicate the rushing water.

Just like sketching any other water body, it's important not to go overboard with drawing these lines, though.

River

River water is not as calm as a lake, but it's calmer than a waterfall.

The shape of the river is what defines it, and its shape can be depicted using its surroundings.

Here the river is shown to be winding its way through the landscape. Notice how the details of the landscape keep getting less and less in the picture. This provides the feel of distance.

Seashore

Seashore can be rocky or flat.

For rocky seashore, waves keep crashing into the rocks, creating dramatic splashes.

When sketching such splashes, we can use stippling to great effect to create the "spray" effect.

On a calm seashore, a patch of wet sand forms where the waves keep advancing and retreating over the land.

This patch of wet, packed sand can be used to sketch interesting reflections.

SHADING
TECHNIQUES
EXERCISE

Now let's use the following reference photograph to do a complete sketch using the techniques we learned.

Before we begin, keep this in mind.

What I am showing you is a guideline. You may follow it for understanding. But this is not the only right way to do sketching.

You may do any kind of variations to the techniques I show you, and you will still be right.

You don't need to exactly copy the photograph. You may take any liberty related to composition, lighting, textures, or anything for that matter.

As I have already said earlier, "This is art, not a freaking Math test!".

Let's begin by dividing the reference photograph into a 3 X 3 grid.

To understand why we do this, we will digress a bit and discuss something called "Rule of Thirds".

Whaaat? There's a rule for sketching? But I had just said a few chapters ago that there are only two rules to sketching? Where did this third rule come from?

Hold your guns, people. It's named as "Rule", but it's only a "rule of thumb".

This "rule" applies to compositions of all kind of visual arts like sketching, painting, photography and even filmmaking, and it's very simple.

A composition looks more pleasant when the main subjects are kept away from the center.

When we click a picture, or sketch a picture, the first impulse is to keep all the interesting things bang in the middle. Avoid this impulse.

Keeping the main subject away from the center creates a slight imbalance in the composition, which draws the viewer's interest.

Do you see the rule of thirds applied in this photograph?

You don't need to do exact division like this, just be aware of it mentally.

You may draw the same grid on the paper where you will be doing the final sketch.

Don't use a ruler to draw this grid! And keep the lines very loose and faint. We will be erasing them later.

Also keep some space marked away from all corners of the paper. You don't want to spill over the paper.

As you may have noticed, most of the sketches that I have included in this book do not have well-defined borders.

Forget what they taught you in school. A sketch neither needs to have a fixed border, nor is it necessary for it to fill the entire sheet of paper.

As I keep repeating throughout this book... White spaces are as important as black lines.

Hmm, now that I am done doling out philosophy, I will make myself useful and actually do what I am supposed to do, that is, tell you how to proceed with the sketch.

We will start with a rough pencil sketch. This sketch is not meant to be very detailed.

The pencil sketch is meant to block in the larger shapes, so we can limit the scope of our sketch.

Here's the outline of the pencil sketch I made prior to pen work.

The lines are sketched thick only for your understanding. In reality, the pencil lines should be so light that they should be visible only to you.

You may observe that in addition to marking the broad shapes, I have marked dark values (with complete blacks / horizontal lines).

Right now, the focus is not on accuracy, but to get the shapes and shadows right.

Remember the chapter "Learning to see"? We are blocking two out of the three elements we discussed in that chapter (shapes and shadows).

We will worry about textures when we do pen work.

Now that the rough sketch is ready, let's look at finishing this sketch using pen work.

For this exercise, I will use technical pens. You are free to use technical pens, or ballpoint/gel pen.

The advantage of technical pens is the freedom to sketch using various tip sizes. But they are not an absolute must.

Keep a white inked ballpoint pen handy for finishing touches. This is optional.

Let's start with pen work.

When doing pen and ink work, it's prudent to start with shapes which are closest to us, as these shapes will overlap others.

I started with this bunch of large leaves in the foreground. As of now, they are not very "polished". But they provide some semblance to the leaves. That's enough for now.

These leaves are drawn with a medium thick (0.3) tip pen.

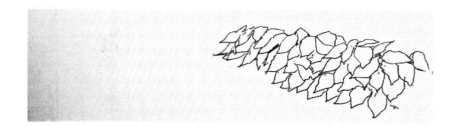

The sketch looks like this as of now

Now we will draw the outline for trees. Since light is falling on the trees from the right side, we will make the left side of the trees slightly darker.

For the left side of the trees, I will be using a 0.3 thick tip pen, while for the right side; I will use 0.1 tip pen. Also note that I have kept the lines randomly broken at places. We can always complete them later. No need to be too precise as of now.

Also note that the trees are slightly "floating" above the ground! This is because we are going to cover the base of trees with some grass, and we need to keep this space empty.

Notice that the lower edge of the shore is drawn holding the clump of leaves we sketched earlier. See how the leaves are overlapping the edge.

Now we will draw the mysterious mini-pillars behind the clump of leaves on the lower right side.

Points to note for drawing these pillars:

The pillars appear to float in the air, as their lower ends will be covered in grass.

For each pillar, some area on the top is marked. This is where the light will fall, creating highlights. We will not make this area dark like rest of the pillar.

Some stones in the water are also sketched. Keep the lower edge of each stone flat, regardless of the overall stone shape.

Here we sketch the grass and some foliage at the far end of the little piece of land.

Notice how the grass is drawn with minimum criss-cross strokes. It's important not to overdo sketching grass. Since the grass is at the far end, its details should be less visible.

The foliage is sketched using random strokes and a thin (0.1) tip pen. Same for grass.

The mini pillars are now completely darkened, except those areas marked for highlights.

Next, we mark the stokes of the palm fronds. Note how the fronds radiate outward from the tree. Stokes ("Spines" of the fronds) of the closer tree are marked thicker.

Now we will complete the details of the palm fronds.

For the fronds directly facing us, we need to sketch the pinnae (leaves) on both sides of the stock. For the fronds facing away, we need to sketch the pinnae on only one side.

There will be a massive, mind-numbing overlap between the fronds. It's ok. One does not need to be too accurate as of now. We can cover up every error later using shading.

Now we will add some texture to the tree trunks. For this, do these two things:

1. Make the left edges of the trees (away from light), very dark with thick pen. Here, I have used a 0.4 tip pen to darken the tree edges.
2. Using horizontal contour strokes, intermittently sketch over the tree trunk. Don't sketch too many strokes. We just need to give a feel of the texture.

Sketch the texture most prominently on the closest of the trees. Do this using a thin lipped pen.

Now darken the undersides of the clump of leaves near the waterline. Use a thicker tip pen/brush tip pen for this.

Now draw a horizontal line indicating the horizon as shown here. This line should be drawn with a thin tip pen, because we are indicating a long distance here.

Draw the faint outline of hills and shrubs over this line using HB pencil. Then carefully draw vertical hatching strokes from horizon line to the pencil line as shown here.

For these hatching strokes, use the thinnest tip pen you have at your disposal.

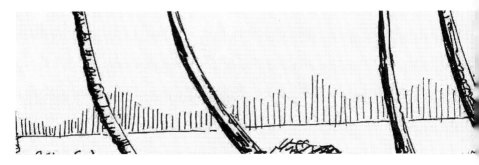

Erase the pencil line after the strokes are completed.

Let's add some reflections in the water.

The reflections nearer to the shore will be very dark. As we move away from the shore, they become gradually lighter (and broken with some white spaces).

Keep some white spaces to indicate breaks in the shadows as shown here.

Some horizontal pen strokes here and there are enough to indicate calm water.

Now our sketch looks like this.

Now it's time to add some finishing touches. I am using a very thin tip pen (Pigma micron 0.005) and a white Uniball ball point pen for finishing touches.

It totally depends on you when you deem your sketch complete. For me, the most difficult part is to decide when a sketch is complete!

One hint - when you feel the sketch is complete, stop right there and get over the urge to overdo it.

Easier said than done, I know!

The completed sketch (for me!) looks like this.

Don't forget to sign it! You have earned it :-)

BEFORE WE PART...

Now that we have learned about so many possibilities for sketching, it's time to apply them in your sketches.

The next few pages contain some of the sketches for your inspiration. There are many more subjects which can be drawn using pens and inks. All of them could not be covered in a single book.

However, I promise that I will be back soon with more books covering more subjects.

I will be more than happy to hear from you. How did you find this book? Which of the additional topics related to pen and ink sketching would you like to see in the near future?

I would also love to see any artworks you created after reading this book.

Thanks for reading, and Happy Sketching :-)

INSPIRATION

Shinsh

GRATITUDE

I am extremely grateful to my wife Aparna, who has consistently stood with me, encouraged me and tolerated me through all my art endeavours and eccentricities.

I am thankful to the following fellow artists, authors and creatives, who reviewed the book manuscript very patiently and came up with suggestions which catapulted the quality of this book by quantum leaps. You guys are incredible.

- Sanjeev Joshi
- Preetam Tiwari
- Shamika Nair
- Deepak Satarkar

Happy Sketching :-)

REQUEST FOR REVIEW

Did you receive any value from this book? Did you enjoy reading it?

If yes, would you please leave a review for this book?

https://www.amazon.com/dp/1725571145

The review will help this book reach more readers worldwide and help them truly enjoy the experience of Pen and Ink Sketching.

After all, the joy multiplies when shared, right :-)?

You are most welcome to send me suggestions and ideas for the next books.

MORE ART GEMS BY SHIRISH

Dozens of FREE art demonstrations are available by Shirish on his YouTube channel: https://www.youtube.com/c/huesandtones

Composition and Perspective

A simple, yet powerful guide to draw stunning, expressive sketches

https://www.amazon.com/dp/B07KVFZ9CC

COMPOSITION and PERSPECTIVE

A simple, yet powerful guide to draw stunning, expressive sketches.

Shirish Deshpande

Learn to draw amazingly fun sketches using the easy-to-use, yet powerful techniques for solid compositions and accurate perspective.

Learn the basics of perspective like the horizon, vanishing point and picture plane.

Learn to sketch using one, two, three, and even five-point perspective!

And that's not all! Along with several artworks, you will find links to FREE video demonstrations where the author shows you exactly how these artworks were created.

Dystopian Encounters - Wave 1

Musings from Another Dimension – An Adult Coloring Book

https://www.amazon.com/dp/1797455028

Welcome to the Musings from Another Dimension, where the surreal meets the real, lines and shapes form out of the deepest recesses of the subconscious, ancient ruins of the lost cities grapple with the encroaching aliens, and beautiful mermaids dance among the corals!

Say goodbye to your stress and prepare to indulge in an exotic coloring adventure.

49997898R00106

Made in the USA
Middletown, DE
22 June 2019